Just Girlfriends

Just Girlfriends
More Than Just Chit-Chat and Chocolate

Bonnie Louise Kuchler

 Willow Creek Press

Published by Willow Creek Press
P.O. Box 147, Minocqua, Wisconsin 54548

Editor: Andrea Donner

Photo Credits: p2 © Jeff Venuda/www.jeffvanugaphotography.com; p6 © John E. Marriott/Alamy; p9 © Juniors Bildarchiv/Alamy; p10 © Robert Pickett/Papilio/Alamy; p13 © Jane Burton/naturepl.com; p14 © Penny Boyd/Alamy; p17 © Petra Wegner/naturepl.com; p18 © Peter Steiner/Alamy; p21 © Brian Elliott/Alamy; p22 © Pete Oxford/Steve Bloom Images/Alamy; p24 © Gary Randall/kimballstock.com; p26 © Ron Kimball/kimballstock.com; p28 © Holger Ehlers/Alamy; p31 © Thorsten Milse/Robert Harding Picture Library Ltd./Alamy; p32 © T.J. Rich/naturepl.com; p35 © Mark J. Barrett/Alamy; p36 © Jane Burton/naturepl.com; p39 © Lisa & Mike Husar/www.teamhusar.com; p40 © Augusto Stanzani/ardea.com; p42 © Arctos Images/Alamy; p45 © Daniel J. Cox/naturalexposures.com; p46 © Juniors Bildarchiv/Alamy; p49 © Petra Wegner/Alamy; p50 © Arco Images/Alamy; p53 © Renee Stockdale/kimballstock.com; p54 © Lisa & Mike Husar/www.teamhusar.com; p57 © Juniors Bildarchiv/Alamy; p58 © Jörn Friederich/imagebroker/Alamy; p60 © Jane Burton/naturepl.com; p63 © Dave Porter/Alamy; p64 © Bill Coster/Alamy; p67 © Juergen & Christine Sohns/Animals Animals/Earch Scenes; p68 © Digital Archive Japan/Alamy; p71 © Lisa & Mike Husar/www.teamhusar.com; p72 © Penny Boyd/Alamy; p75 © Anup Shah/naturepl.com; p76 © Schmidbauer/blickwinkel/Alamy; p78 © Roger Cracknell 01/Classic/Alamy; p81 © John Giustina/Digital Vision/Alamy; p82 © Steve Bloom Images/Alamy; p85 © Mark Taylor/naturepl.com; p86 © John Daniels/Ardea.com; p89 © Jane Burton/naturepl.com; p90 © Lisa & Mike Husar/www.teamhusar.com; p93 © Jane Burton/naturepl.com; p94 © Pete Oxford/naturepl.com

Printed in Canada

Some things only girlfriends understand—

Girlfriends understand our language. They don't require a
logical translation each time we gush, blurt, rant, or sigh.

They understand that a "balanced" meal can include
a diet drink and a fudge brownie à la mode.

Girlfriends understand we can never trust
dressing-room mirrors or bathroom scales.

And they understand we need them as mirrors, cushions,
cheering squads, and ever-ready chocolate co-conspirators.

Girlfriend, this book is for you—
the one whose ear, clothes closet, refrigerator,
and heart are always open.

A Friendship Sprouts

You don't plan to meet a best friend.

Serendipity plucks two unsuspecting people from

their paths, aims them down a new road,

and lights their way with a shared passion or pain.

To have someone we can laugh with is a great gift.

———

George & Karen Grant
American authors

You fall into friendships like a cool lake on a hot,

airless day, or wrap them around you like a blanket

in front of a flaming fire on a bitter night.

———

Lenore Skomal
American author

Friends are those special people we do life with.

———

Editor of Harvest House Publishers

The music of those first friendships

is always playing somewhere in the background

as we go to other dances, other parties.

———

Lois Wyse
American author

I'm tired of doing things with people.

What I want is someone to do nothing with.

———

Martin Edelston
Entrepreneur, publisher and author

Every friend fills a different role.

There are friends...

who will support you on your new diet

and friends who will help you cheat on it.

———

A friend doesn't go on a diet when you are fat...
A friend will tell you she saw your old boyfriend
—and he's a priest.

Erma Bombeck
American humorist

For women, shopping is therapy.

But too much therapy calls for comfort food.

And too much comfort has just one remedy—

an equally comfortable girlfriend.

———

Bonnie Louise Kuchler
American author

The Care & Keeping of Girlfriends

When you bottle up anger,

girlfriends pry open your steam vent,

knowing you'll feel much better

after you've hissed for a while.

There's a big difference between men and girlfriends.

A girlfriend knows who she is listening to—

whether it's you, or your PMS alter ego.

———

Bonnie Louise Kuchler
American author

When you are heavy laden with PMS poundage,

I will deny your girth...

When your jeans no longer fit,

I will reassure you that your dryer is too hot.

———

Cathy Hamilton
American Author

Revealing an embarrassing moment to a girlfriend—

and then laughing about it with her—

is like removing the stinger from a stalker bee.

———

Bonnie Louise Kuchler
American author

When I have opened my heart to a friend,

I am more myself than ever.

———

Thomas Moore
American author

The closer two girlfriends get,

the more they behave like sisters.

That can be good or bad,

depending on the sister.

———

Bonnie Louise Kuchler
American author

Sometimes good friends have bad days.

———

Lois Wyse
American author

One may be my very good friend,

and yet not of my opinion.

———

Margaret Cavendish
Duchess of Newcastle

The essence of true friendship is to
make allowance for another's little lapses.

———

David Storey
English playwright

Without Girlfriends
We Would Wither

Girlfriends know that when your heart rips open,

you can't sew it together by yourself.

They also know which ailments

can be cured with chocolate, and which require hugs.

Where would you be in your life without your girlfriends?

They sustain you, right you,

harbor you, laugh with you, and love you.

———

Lenore Skomal
American author

With whom but a girlfriend can you...

blubber with guaranteed consolation...

change your mind without explanation...

recite endless details with no point?

———

Joy MacKenzie
American author

The friend who holds your hand

and says the wrong thing

is made of dearer stuff

than the one who stays away.

———

Barbara Kingsolver
American author

Few comforts are more alluring for a woman

than the rich, intimate territory of women's talk.

A woman friend will say, "You are not alone.

I have felt that way, too. This is what happened to me."

Home, in other words.

———

Elsa Walsh
American author

How much it hurts when a friend moves away—

and leaves behind only silence.

———

Pam Brown
American author

A day without a friend is like a pot

without a single drop of honey left inside.

———

Winnie the Pooh (A. A. Milne)

Our friends know our danger spots—

the places where the bridge goes out most often—

and help shore us up.

———

Carmen Renee Berry and Tamara Traeder
American authors

Nobody, but nobody, can make it out here alone.

———

Dr. Maya Angelou
American writer, educator, civil rights activist

Girlfriends Stand
Strong in Storms

You don't need to ask girlfriends for help.

Their antennas are fully extended,

catching your unspoken signals.

When times are bad and we lose ourselves,

our girlfriends know where to find us.

———

Karen Neuburger
American author

A real friend never gets in your way,

unless you happen to be on the way down.

———

Eric Hoffer
American philosopher and author

Girlfriends share two ageless elixirs:

We laugh until we cry,

and we cry until we laugh.

Either one heals us from the inside out.

———

Bonnie Louise Kuchler
American author

So long as you can sweeten another's pain,

life is not in vain.

———

Helen Keller
American author

When we do not have the strength within ourselves,

our girlfriends loan us their hope, their passion...

so that on borrowed faith, we can take the next step.

———

Carmen Renee Berry & Tamara Traeder
American authors

I often think, how could I have survived

without these women?

———

Claudette Renner
Quoted in *Chicken Soup for the Soul: Life Lessons for Women*

A clutch of girlfriends is warmth.

A pack of them is near invincibility.

———

Bonnie Louise Kuchler
American author

Indeed, we do not really live

unless we have friends surrounding us like

a firm wall against the winds of the world.

———

Charles Hanson Towne
American poet

Friendship in Full Bloom

A girlfriend keeps your most intimate secrets.

She's like a safe deposit box,

storing your irreplaceable valuables.

Best friends can practically speak with their eyes—

just a knowing glance speaks a thousand words.

———

John Sage

A friend is one who sees through you
and still enjoys the view.

———

Wilma Askinas
American writer

Certain flaws are necessary...

It would seem strange if old friends

lacked certain quirks.

———

Johann Wolfgang von Goethe
German author and playwright

Just thinking about a friend

makes you want to do a happy dance,

because a friend is someone who loves you

in spite of your faults.

———

Charles M. Schulz
American cartoonist

I have learned that to be with those I like is enough.

———

Walt Whitman
American poet

Sometimes only a gentle silence,

between two friends,

can speak the tenderness we feel.

———

Joan Walsh Anglund
American author and illustrator

You could search the whole world

looking for a friendship like ours,

And you would only wear out a good pair of feet.

———

Bradley Trevor Grieve
Australian author

Let's make our friendship last until

our hair is gray and we talk too loud...

———

Kathy L. Lobdell
Quoted in *Girlfriends: A Celebration of the Special
Friendships Shared Between Women*